WHY YOU'RE
100%

wonderful

WHAT'S BETTER THAN THE BEST?

≋ YOU! ≋

YOUR FRIENDSHIP, YOUR SPIRIT, YOUR PERSONALITY... EVERYTHING YOU ARE IS WITHOUT EQUAL, AND I'M SO DARN LUCKY TO KNOW YOU. WHICH IS WHY I'VE PUT TOGETHER THIS LITTLE BOOK OF ALL THE THINGS I ADMIRE MOST ABOUT YOU.

DO YOU KNOW THAT I *love* BEING ON YOUR SIDE?

IF OUR FRIENDSHIP WERE A SPORTS TEAM, OUR NAME WOULD BE...

the

write team
name here

THERE ARE ONLY GOOD MOMENTS WHEN *you're* AROUND.

HERE'S WHAT TIME FEELS LIKE WITH YOU...

draw the hour and minute hands

IT'S EASY TO SEE
YOU'RE EQUAL PARTS...

and

IT'S THE PERFECT BALANCE.

YOU'RE REALLY

remarkable.

YOU REMIND ME, JUST BY BEING

————————————————————————

HOW HAPPY I AM THAT
WE'RE FRIENDS.

YOUR WONDERFULNESS IS OTHERWORLDLY.

IF YOU WERE A MAGICAL CREATURE, YOU'D HAVE...

☐ A FLUFFY TAIL

☐ COLORFUL WINGS

☐ MAJESTIC HORNS

☐ GRACEFUL FINS

- ☐ SHINING SCALES
- ☐ SUPER-SOFT FUR
- ☐ PEARLESCENT FEATHERS
- ☐ A VOLUMINOUS MANE

- ☐ A HEART OF GOLD
- ☐ AN UNMATCHED MIND
- ☐ A TALENT FOR ELOQUENCE
- ☐ A SPIRIT THAT COMFORTS OTHERS

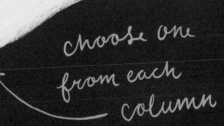

choose one from each column

I ADMIRE HOW TALENTED
YOU ARE AT SO MANY
THINGS. LIKE HOW YOU CAN...

YOU'RE
COMPLETELY
delightful.

ALL THE TIME, I THINK
ABOUT HOW

YOU ARE.
(and it makes me smile)

OUR FRIENDSHIP HAS THE BEST QUALITIES...

LOYALTY

LAUGHTER

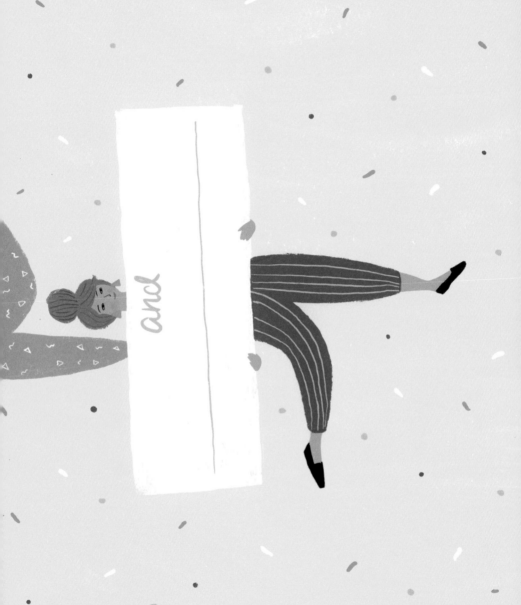

NO MATTER WHAT, WE
HAVE NO TROUBLE HAVING
A GOOD TIME.

MY MOST FAVORITE WAY
WE SPEND TIME TOGETHER
has to be...

- [ ] GOING ON BIG ADVENTURES
- [ ] STAYING IN AND TALKING ABOUT *everything*
- [ ] GETTING DINNER AND CATCHING UP
- [ ] EXPERIENCING NEW THINGS
- [ ] _____

AND IF THE WORLD
GETS US DOWN,
I KNOW I CAN RELY
ON *your*...

_____

_____

_____

(THANK YOU FOR BEING THE
ONE WHO HELPS GET ME THROUGH.)

YOU'RE
BEYOND
brilliant.

I REALIZE, QUITE OFTEN,
HOW GOOD YOU ARE AT

_____

1 part _____

_____

2 parts _____

_____

4 parts _____

_____

SAVORY
SINCERITY

WELL-SEASONED
WISDOM

SCRUMPTIOUS
STRENGTH

HEAVENLY
HONESTY

YOU HAVE ALL THE RIGHT INGREDIENTS TOO.

AND IT'S SO NICE
HOW YOU'RE NOT LIKE
ANYONE ELSE.

THESE ARE ONLY A
FEW THINGS THAT MAKE
YOU SO UNIQUE...

YOU'RE TRULY

incredible.

I'M PARTICULARY IN AWE

OF THE WAY YOU

_ _.

(it's kind of too good to be true)

0 ← HAPPINESS → 100%

BEFORE I MET YOU

AFTER I MET YOU

KNOWING WE WILL always BE FRIENDS

(color in the graph)

AND ON A SCALE OF
ONE TO AWESOME, YOU'D
DEFINITELY RANK AS...

- ☐ PRETTY DARN AWESOME
- ☐ SUPERBLY GREAT
- ☐ TOO IMPRESSIVE FOR WORDS
- ☐ ABSOLUTELY PERFECT
- ☐ RIDICULOUSLY WONDERFUL

I HOPE YOU KNOW YOU
CONSISTENTLY ADD UP TO
SOMETHING *good.*

YOU'RE VERY

extraordinary.

HONESTLY, SOMETIMES I CAN'T
BELIEVE HOW ABSOLUTELY

— — — — — — — — — — — — —

YOU ARE.

THINKING ABOUT IT, IF YOU WERE ONE OF THE SEASONS,

YOU'D HAVE TO BE...

(color in a cat)

WINTER

SPRING

BECAUSE YOU'RE SO

_____

_____.

SUMMER

≈ FALL ≈

---

you MAKE EVERY
MOMENT SWEET.

IN FACT, IF YOU WERE
A SPECIAL DRINK, I'D SAY
YOU WOULD BE...

MENU

- ☐ A REFINED RASPBERRY TEA
- ☐ AN ELEGANT LAVENDER LATTE
- ☐ A PERKY HAZELNUT HOT CHOCOLATE
- ☐ _____

YOU'RE
ALTOGETHER
Amazing.

I APPRECIATE HOW
YOU ALWAYS MAKE OTHERS
(and me!) FEEL SO

_ _ _ _ _ _ _ _ _ _ _ _ _ _ _ _ _ _ _

THE GALAXY SHINES
BRIGHTER BECAUSE
OF you.

_____
adjective

_____
color

_____
Greek alphabet letter

SEE? THIS NEWFOUND
Star IS EVEN NAMED
AFTER YOU.

YES! IT'S CONFIRMED.

THE WHOLE UNIVERSE
KNOWS IT, AND I KNOW
IT TOO.

YOU'RE

SIMPLY

COMPENDIUM.
live inspired

Written by: Amelia Riedler
Illustrated by: Jill Labieniec
Edited by: Kristin Eade

Library of Congress Control Number: 2021944304 | ISBN: 978-1-970147-70-4

1st printing. Printed in China with soy inks on FSC®-Mix certified paper.

Create meaningful moments with gifts that inspire.

CONNECT WITH US
live-inspired.com | sayhello@compendiuminc.com

    @compendiumliveinspired
#compendiumliveinspired